Mark Pettinelli

EMOTION
LOGIC
PERCEPTION
Thoughts
Ideas
CONCEPTS
INTENTIONS

AF254799

Mark Rettinelli

EMOTIONS are

unconscious

Compared to

Thoughts

Thoughts can
be about Ideas or
concepts

Mark Rettinelli

Mark Rettinelli

LOGIC is about

Thinking Clearly

and with Reasoning

versus thinking in

a disordered Fashion

Clarity and Sense

Mark Rettinelli

Mark Petanella

FEELINGS

EMOTIONS are stronger than FEELINGS

Also, FEELINGS are more sensory like taste, touch, sight, sound and smell

Mark Petanella

Mark Pettinella

Logic is about thinking clearly

thoughts can be
about ideas or concepts

IDEAS

CONCEPTS

THOUGHTS

Mark Pettinella

Mark Pettinelli

Logic is
about thinking
CLEARLY

For instance,
I could be thinking
about A

CONCEPT

Mark Pettinelli

Mark Rettinelli

**If you think
with LOGIC**

Then you think
About stuff
That makes
Sense and is
Clear

Mark Rettinelli

Mark Pettinelli

Feeling are about things you can <u>Feel</u>

while thoughts are about things you <u>THINK</u>

Mark Pettinelli

Mark Pettinella

FEELINGS

are different from

THOUGTS thoughts

Thoughts are things you can <u>think</u> about while feelings are things you <u>feel</u>

Mark Pettinella

Mark Kettinella

The Mind creates representations
Of the world

that we can act on
from within the mind

The point of creating representations
is to achieve goals

the mind enables us
to Act and achieve
GOALS

Mark Kettinella

Mark Pettinelli

Some decisions can be
<u>deliberate</u> and <u>intentional</u>

That means it is a deliberate
and conscious decision

while, on the other hand,
a decision or action could be
done more by mistake,
automatically, or without
thinking making it be
more <u>unconscious</u>

Mark Pettinelli

Marc Pettinelli

Some EMOTIONS

Happy	Annoyance
Sad	Pride
Anger	Envy Gratitude
Fear	Lust
Disgust	Confusion
Anxiety	Jealousy
Embarrassment	Boredom
Shame	Amusement
Surprise	Loneliness
Love	Enthusiasm
	Contempt
Satisfaction	Shyness

Marc Pettinelli

Mark Pettinelli

Decisions and Actions

can be

<u>instinctual</u> or

<u>deliberate</u>

if an action or decision is
is from instinct then it
could be more unconscious
than a decision that is more
<u>deliberate</u>

Mark Pettinelli

Mario Bettinelli

The Mind controls <u>Mental</u>
<u>functions</u> such as:

Perception

Attention

Memory

Emotions

Language

deciding, thinking
and Reasoning

Mario Bettinelli

Mark Pettinelli

Emotions are also
primary like

Happy or Sad
or Anger or disgust

While feelings are

simply anything we

can feel, including the

senses

Mark Pettinelli

Mark Pettinelli

the progression of processing from lower to higher areas of the brain is called hierarchical processing

Neurons send signals to higher areas of the brain to form more complex representations or images

Mark Pettinelli

Mark Pettinelli

Concepts fit into
categories that can be
similar or different
for instance a <u>dog</u> could have
typical features of <u>dogs</u>

Your mind would categorize
that dog you see as a typical
dog, also the dog has features
similar to other animals

Mark Pettinelli

Mark Pettinelli

Logical Ideas

Perceptions, Actions

Representations and

Visual and Mental Images

Reasoning and thinking

Concepts and Categories

Mark Pettinelli

www.ingramcontent.com/pod-product-compliance
Lightning Source LLC
Chambersburg PA
CBHW042146030726
47599CB00002B/637